Presidential Leaders

FAMOUS FRIENDS

by
Jerry Aten

illustrated by Judy Hierstein

Cover by Tom Foster

Copyright © Good Apple, Inc., 1986

ISBN No. 0-86653-347-8

Printing No. 98765

GOOD APPLE, INC.
BOX 299
CARTHAGE, IL 62321-0299

Presidential Leaders

TABLE OF CONTENTS

INTRODUCTION

Working with young children and history is not at all difficult. Certainly one would never assume that young children could sit and recite critical facts—that Thomas Jefferson was born in 1743, that he wrote the Declaration of Independence, designed his own beautiful home Monticello and created the plan for the University of Virginia. However, when all this is woven into a historical story, children will listen, and they will remember many things that become more meaningful with time and growth.

HISTORY CAN BECOME REAL

As we talk with the children about historical facts and fun happenings, we need to realize that children learn about the past before they learn about the future. It's much easier to say to a young child something happened yesterday than it is to say that it will happen tomorrow. Since it has happened to them, they understand.

As we begin to look at goals that are typically set for young children in social studies, we find that they start with the self, extend into family friends, school, community, cities, states and even countries. However, a closer examination of the curricula would suggest that we also should present material on human dignity, respect for human life, an appreciation for the rights of others, survival, interdependence, economy, making choices, ethnicity, relating to others, and the uniqueness of all individuals.

IN THIS BOOK YOU WILL FIND:

Factual stories about famous Presidents that can be read to young children.

Suggestions to adults on presenting the stories' related activities.

A suggested time line for use in the classroom that will help children relate to time in history.

Vocabulary and discussion questions for use with the stories.

A list of follow-up activities.

Additional facts to present to the children.

Markers or symbols for a map to be placed in your room to show children where things happened in relation to where they are.

A list of additional resources.

A work sheet for each President to be reproduced for each child to be used either as a take-home activity or in-class activity sheet.

Presidential Leaders was designed to bring to young children important information about its most well-remembered Presidents. The order of their presentation is chronological. The presentation you choose to use with your children may be based on seasonal or other personal preference.

TIME LINES

Use an entire wall for the classroom time line. This "line" for young children should not look like this one below.

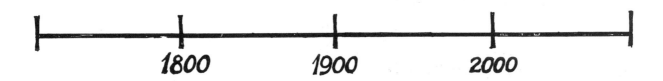

It is suggested that you use a piece of butcher paper 2′ tall and the length of the room that can be written on, printed on and has plenty of room for students' "art." Use a section on the time line for the 1900's, one for the 1800's, and one for the 1700's.

Many things will happen during the school year that can be placed on the time line. For example:

1. Take a picture of your class and place it at the present.

2. Have the children bring pictures of themselves when they were babies, and place these on the time line on the year they were born.

3. Have children bring pictures of their parents and place these to mark the years of their parents' births.

4. Children may have photos at home of historical events. You can place these on the appropriate dates.

5. Before you start this series of stories, brainstorm with children and ask them what they know about what happened a long time ago. Place some of these events on the time line.

6. Allow children to project what might happen years from now. Place these events off the end of the time line.

KIDS' BOOKS

Included in this book are pages that may be cut out or duplicated to make a book to read to the kids. All you need to do is fold the three pages together. If you have access to a copy machine and wish to make a booklet for each child, simply run the desired number of copies through the machine. Then turn over both the original and the copies and run through the machine again.

On the back of each book are the new vocabulary words and a list of other resources.

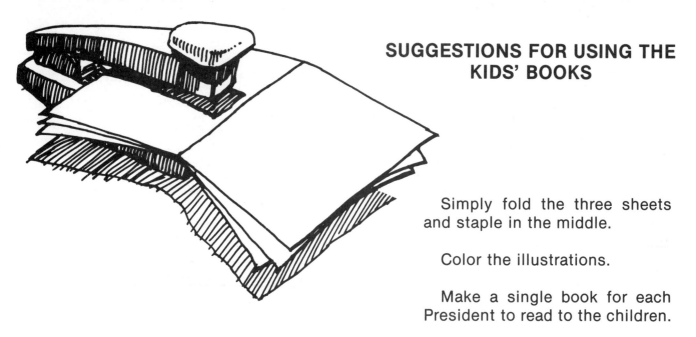

SUGGESTIONS FOR USING THE KIDS' BOOKS

Simply fold the three sheets and staple in the middle.

Color the illustrations.

Make a single book for each President to read to the children.

Make several booklets of each story; then tape the story and place in a listening center with earphones.

Make enough copies for each child in the class to use at school and to take home to share with his parents.

Use the books as supplemental reading.

SUGGESTIONS FOR THE WORK SHEETS

Each work sheet has a picture of a FAMOUS FRIEND at the top and six squares at the bottom. Each square is a cue to an interesting fact about the life of the FAMOUS FRIEND. The work sheets can be used in a variety of ways. The following list has been placed in the order of difficulty with easier things for younger children coming first.

Color the pictures on the page. Place them all in a folder, and take them home to share with parents. Make covers for them.

Color and cut out all the squares at the bottoms of the pages and laminate. Use the cards for games. Each child chooses one and guesses who fits the cue.

Cut out the pictures and put them in order of presentation in the story.

Color, cut out and paste the square on a 3" x 6" piece of paper. Write the one-word cue on the right side.

Color, cut out and paste the square in the corner of a 6" x 9" piece of paper. Write an explanation of how the cue relates to the FAMOUS FRIEND.

George Washington

George Washington was born in 1732 in Virginia. His parents named him George after the King of England. King George ruled over Colonial Virginia.

His parents were very wealthy, and George grew up on a large tobacco *plantation*. He played with his three brothers and his sister on the plantation. When he was six years old, his family moved to another plantation. George was excited about his new home.

Vocabulary

plantation

colonies

responsibility

guidance

widow

free

surveyors

Resources

Meet George Washington, Heilbroner.

George Washington, Graff.

George Washington, Stevenson (Childhood of Famous Americans Series).

George Washington, Foster.

Notes to Adults

One of the most popular times to talk to children about George Washington is in February when they can see his silhouette hanging in many card shops and classrooms.

Founders, another book in this series, deals with people who can be tied in with George Washington: Betsy Ross, Paul Revere and Benjamin Franklin. One of the Presidents frequently seen with Washington is Lincoln, since both have birthdays celebrated in February.

The children are learning to recognize the silhouette of Washington as Washington, and this is placed on the time line at the time of his life.

After the war, George went back to Mount Vernon to be with Martha and farm the plantation he loved so well, but he was needed by his country because he was a good leader. He was asked to become the new country's first President. So he gave up his quiet life and served his country once again. George served his country well. He became known as the Father of Our Country.

He could go down by the river and watch the big ships load and unload. The ships came from England. On board were clothes and dishes and tools and toys and other things. When the ships were empty, the workers began putting barrels of tobacco on them. The tobacco was used like money in Virginia.

George led his men through a long hard war with England. One cold winter his army was camped at Valley Forge. The British army was nearby in the city of Philadelphia, where they were warm and comfortable. George's men were hungry and cold, and they needed clothes and medicine. But they stayed through the winter and they won the war. The colonies were free.

George had an older brother named Lawrence who taught him many things. Lawrence was trained to be a soldier. He taught George what he knew and George practiced very hard. The practice would someday make him a good soldier.

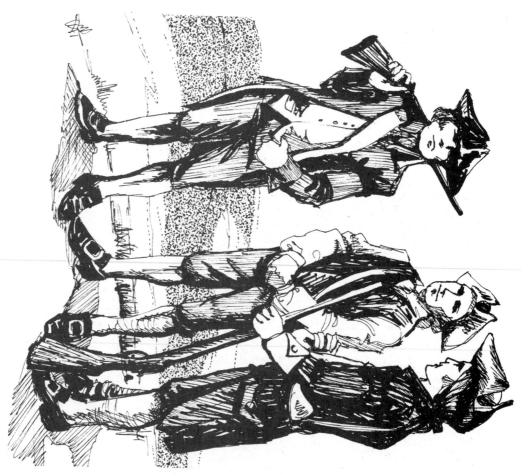

The leaders of the colonies knew that George had learned how to be a good soldier from his brother Lawrence. They asked him to become a leader in the army. George wanted to stay home on his plantation with Martha and his family. But he knew how important it was to win the war, so he decided to help. He became a leader in the army.

When George was eleven years old, his father died. George had to take on the *responsibility* of helping to run their plantation called Mount Vernon. He looked to Lawrence for *guidance*. Lawrence and George worked together so that their plantation would continue to grow.

Virginia and the other *colonies* that belonged to England decided they wanted to be *free*. The leaders asked King George to let them be free, but the King said, "No." So the leaders of the colonies decided that the only way to be free was to fight a war with England. This war was called the American Revolution.

One day George and his friends were watching a team of *surveyors* near Fredericksburg. He remembered that his father had some surveying instruments. George went home and found them, and he decided he wanted to become a surveyor. He studied very hard and learned to be a good surveyor. George became friends with Lord Fairfax, who was a wealthy landowner. He got a job surveying the land owned by Lord Fairfax.

George saved most of the money he earned. When he was eighteen, he bought a big plantation of his own. When his brother Lawrence died, he left the plantation Mount Vernon to George. He returned to farming. Then he married a *widow* named Martha Custis who had two children, Patsy and Jack. George became their father.

Questions and Activities

GEORGE WASHINGTON

Discussion Questions

1. Do you know what a President does? Who knows who the President of the United States is now?

2. Have you ever been on a tobacco farm? What can you tell us about growing tobacco? Why don't we use tobacco for money today?

3. George practiced for a long time in order to become a good soldier. Is there something you want to be when you grow up? What is it that you want to be? What can you do now to get ready to be that when you grow up?

4. George wanted to stay on his plantation and farm, but he went to help fight to win the war instead. Why do you think he did this? Why was it so important to him to have the colonies win the war with England?

5. What do you do when you are cold or hungry? What would it be like if you couldn't do that?

6. Why do you think we call George Washington the Father of Our Country?

Activities

1. Be sure to place George on the time line and on the map.

2. Place a silhouette of George Washington on your bulletin board. Then make a silhouette of each child and place those on the board as well.

3. Show children flags of the thirteen separate colonies and of the first flag all of them used as part of the United States of America. Then compare with them the flag as we know it today. Show them a map of the thirteen original colonies and discuss with them the reasons for their eastern location. Then show them a map of the United States as we know it today.

4. Celebrate the birthday of George Washington on February 22. Have a birthday cake decorated with red, white and blue icing. While the children are eating their cake, play for them patriotic songs of America—songs like "The Star-Spangled Banner," "God Bless America" and "America." Conclude your George Washington party by teaching them the Pledge of Allegiance.

THE FATHER OF OUR COUNTRY

GEORGE WASHINGTON

Thomas Jefferson

Thomas Jefferson was born in Virginia in 1743. His father owned a plantation and was a member of the House of Burgesses. His mother came from a wealthy family. She was a member of Virginia's high *society*.

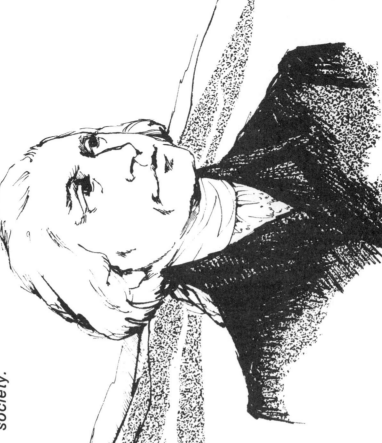

During his boyhood Tom enjoyed fishing and swimming in the streams. He liked to hunt in the woods, too. This kind of free living gave him a feeling of *independence*. He felt that all people are born equal and should have the right to be independent.

1

Vocabulary

society
treaties
inherited
independence
opposite
resolution
courage

Resources

Thomas Jefferson, Father of Democracy, Sheean.
Tom Jefferson, Boy of Colonial Days, Monsell.

12

Notes to Adults

It was Thomas Jefferson who planned the Declaration of Independence; therefore, any time the nation's freedom from England is discussed is an appropriate time to feature the material on his life. While the document itself contains language beyond the limited vocabularies of children, there are a few key words and phrases that can be explained that will help them understand the meaning of our most precious document.

Jefferson was also an inventor, and this is an excellent time to talk about inventors and their inventions. Showing children the results of Jefferson's genius adds importance to his contribution toward the building of America.

Discussion of the vocabulary words and a well-planned presentation of the question/activity section will bring history alive for the young minds. Thomas Jefferson was indeed one of our greatest Presidents.

2

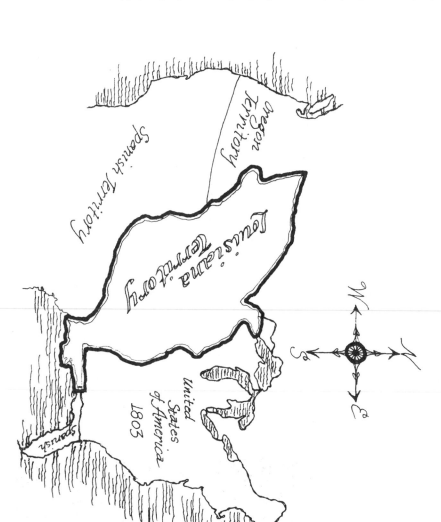

Thomas ran for President in 1800. He won in a very close election over Aaron Burr. President Jefferson did many good things for our country during his two terms as President. He is best remembered for buying all of Louisiana for the United States from France. Louisiana was all the land between the Mississippi River and the Rocky Mountains. The land cost only five million dollars and it doubled the size of the United States.

11

10

Thomas' father died when he was fourteen years old. Tom *inherited* his father's farm and he became the head of the family. This made him grow up faster than most boys his age.

FEDERALISTS

DEMOCRATIC REPUBLICANS

In 1787 he went to Paris to help make *treaties* with European nations. After five years he returned to America and became Secretary of State. He later became Vice President under John Adams. There was only one political party at that time. Thomas and Alexander Hamilton held *opposite* political views. They were both powerful men and both had people to follow them. The result was that we began having a two-party system.

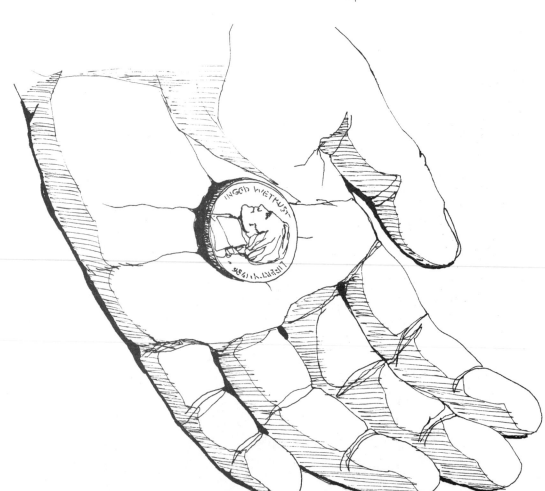

Tom went to college when he was only sixteen. He learned to play the violin. He also listened to conversations between men who were important. Thomas was popular with the other students. He enjoyed dancing and having a good time. He also loved to ride horses.

4

Thomas served as governor of Virginia until after the Revolution. Then we went back to farming. When his wife Martha died, he returned to politics. He served in Congress. While he was there, he created the money system we use which has one hundred pennies in a dollar.

9

12

It took a lot of *courage* for the colonists to declare themselves free. They knew they would have to fight for their freedom. Many people thought the British troops would win easily. But the colonists fought very hard. Finally they won their freedom. The thirteen colonies became the United States of America.

13

After college he studied law very hard. Thomas began to debate with others about the colonies becoming free from England. Thomas Jefferson felt that all men should be free.

When he was twenty-nine, he married a wealthy young widow named Martha Skelton. He brought her to live in his beautiful home called Monticello. Thomas designed the hilltop mansion himself. It is one of the most beautiful homes anywhere. Jefferson also designed many of the buildings at the University of Virginia.

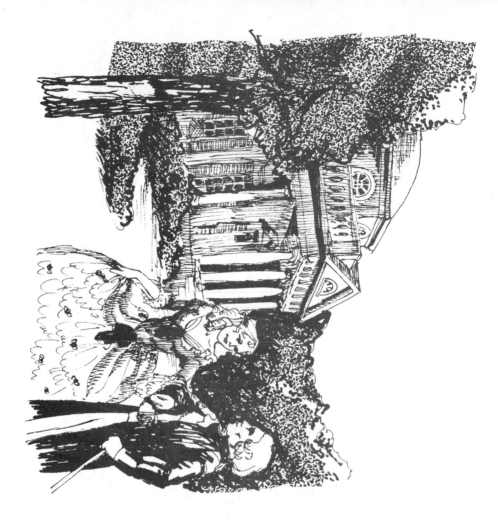

Thomas had trouble giving speeches, but he was a good writer. He was asked to write the *resolution* that would make the colonies free from England. It told King George why the colonists must be free. It was called the Declaration of Independence. He believed in every word he wrote. When he was finished writing it, he sent it to Congress. They discussed it and approved it. Then they sent it to King George.

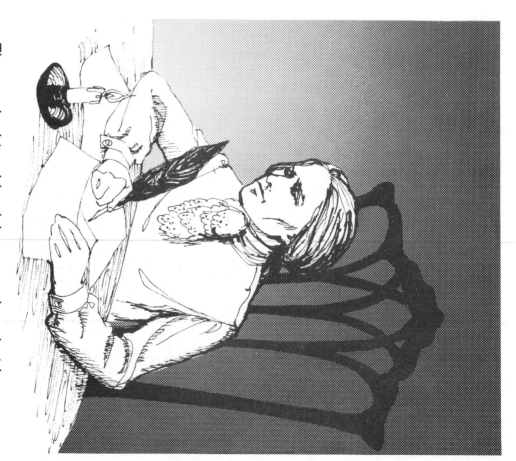

Questions and Activities

THOMAS JEFFERSON

Discussion Questions

1. Do you know what it means to be free? How is being free different from not being free? When have you felt like you were free? Have you ever felt like you weren't free?

2. When Thomas was a boy, he learned to love the great outdoors. How do you think this helped him to love freedom?

3. Why was it so important for the colonists to be free from the rule of King George?

4. Why was Thomas Jefferson chosen to write the Declaration of Independence?

5. Thomas Jefferson wanted to buy Louisiana very much. For what reasons do you think he wanted to get the land for the United States?

6. Jefferson sent Lewis and Clark into Louisiana to see what the country had bought. What would be some of the things Thomas probably told them to be looking for?

Activities

1. Place Thomas Jefferson on the time line and on the map.

2. Thomas Jefferson was one of our greatest Americans. He was an inventor, a lawyer, an architect and a statesman, as well as a good writer. Ask children if they know what each term means and talk with them about some of Jefferson's accomplishments in each area.

3. Place a copy of the Declaration of Independence on your bulletin board. Talk with the children about the importance of this hallowed document and what it meant to the colonists.

4. Bring in one hundred pennies and a one-dollar bill. Explain to children the value of the two. Ask them which they would rather have. Discuss with them the reasons for having both denominations and explain the system developed by Jefferson.

5. The phrase "life, liberty and the pursuit of happiness" is among the most famous in American history. Make those words the title of a bulletin board and place a few pictures on the board that illustrate the freedoms. After discussing them with the children, have them bring in pictures they feel will illustrate the same words. Make a collage of all the pictures for lasting appeal.

6. Show the children a historical map that outlines Louisiana. Compare its size with the rest of the United States as it was known at that time. Explain the advantages of doubling its size.

Abraham Lincoln

Abraham Lincoln was born on February 12, 1809, in a backwoods cabin in Kentucky. His parents were poor farmers. They always looked for new land that would make their lives better.

1

When Abe was seven years old, his family moved to a farm near Pigeon Creek in Indiana. He helped his father Tom cut the trees off the land so they could farm. They also built a log cabin. Tom liked to hunt in the woods. Sometimes he took Abe with him.

Vocabulary

stepmother
ferryboat
legislature
slavery
comfort
debates
punish

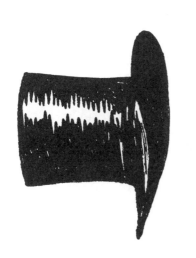

Resources

Lincoln: His Words & His World, Michael P. Dineen.
Abraham Lincoln, Genevieve Foster.

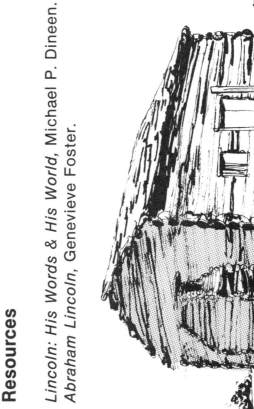

12

17

Notes to Adults

February is also a good month to highlight material about Abraham Lincoln since his date of birth was on February 12. Lincoln and Washington can be studied together as two of our greatest Presidents.

Their silhouettes often provide decorations for February parties and special occasions. Red mats with white silhouettes make an attractive combination when featuring Lincoln and Washington. Children will recognize the differences between the two.

They will also enjoy the activity sheet on Lincoln that can be used in a variety of ways. As always, be certain to fill in the time line to give children a perspective on time.

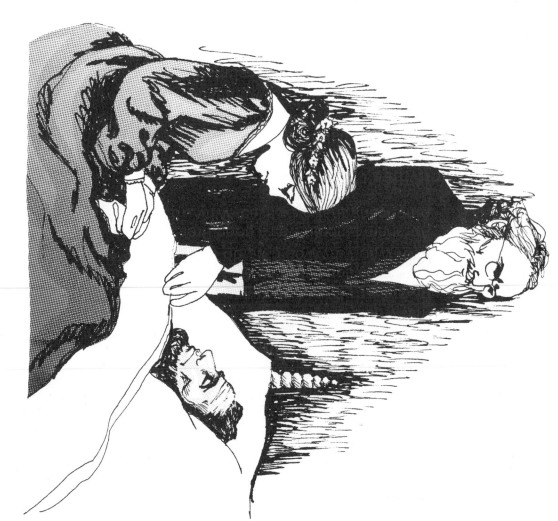

Some people from the North felt that President Lincoln was too kind to the South. They wanted him to *punish* the South for what it had done. On April 14, 1865, President Lincoln was shot by one of these angry men while he was attending a play. He died the next morning. The nation had lost one of its greatest Presidents ever.

Abe's mother Nancy became ill with milk fever when Abraham was only nine years old. He tried to *comfort* her and make her well, but she died. Abraham and his sister Sarah and his father were very sad. Abe wished very much he could read so he could read from the Bible when they buried his mother. He knew she would have liked that. He decided then that he would learn to read.

The North finally won the war. President Lincoln made the decision to make slavery against the law. All slaves had to be set free. After the war President Lincoln was kind to the South who had lost. He wanted to rebuild what had been destroyed.

Abe and Sarah became very close when their father went back to Kentucky to look for a new wife. Tom Lincoln came back married to a very nice lady named Sarah Bush Johnston. She became the step-*mother* to Abe and Sarah. She had three children of her own. She became Abe's best friend and sent him to school so he could learn to read. As soon as Abe finished his work, he would read any book he could find. Abe was very strong. He split logs for three days to earn the money to buy his first book. It was a book about George Washington.

While Abraham was President, the country became divided. People in the South who wanted to allow slavery fought against people in the North who were against it. This was called the Civil War. It was a long and bitter war. It made President Lincoln very sad to think that Americans were killing each other.

VOLUNTEERS WANTED!

1776! 1861!

AN ATTACK UPON WASHINGTON ANTICIPATED!!!!

THE COUNTRY TO THE RESCUE

A REGIMENT FOR SERVICE OF THE UNITED STATES

IS BEING FORMED IN JEFFERSON COUNTY

UNDER THE FLAG

NOW IS THE TIME TO BE ENROLLED!

Abe worked as a hired man on farms until he was seventeen. Then he built a *ferryboat* that took people who wanted to get on the passing steamboats to the middle of the river. Once a ferryboat company from Kentucky had him arrested because they said he couldn't run a ferryboat across the river. The judge told him it was okay to run his boat because the law said he had the right to go to the middle of the river. This made Abraham want to study the law and become a lawyer.

5

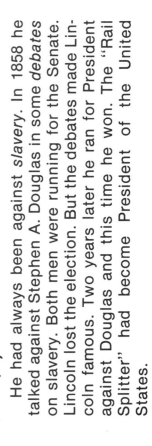

He had always been against *slavery*. In 1858 he talked against Stephen A. Douglas in some *debates* on slavery. Both men were running for the Senate. Lincoln lost the election. But the debates made Lincoln famous. Two years later he ran for President against Douglas and this time he won. The "Rail Splitter" had become President of the United States.

8

21

When Abe was twenty-one, his sister Sarah died giving birth to a child. Abe's father decided it was time to move again. This time they moved to Illinois. He helped his father split rails for fences and build another log cabin. He then went to live in New Salem, on the Sangamon River. Here he worked as a clerk in a general store. Abe was very honest. He always gave customers a full measure. One day he made a mistake and didn't give a lady enough tea. He wrapped up the rest of the tea and walked four miles to take it to her!

6

In 1834 he was elected to the state *legislature.* Abe became engaged to Ann Rutledge. He had been fond of her for a long time. But Ann died. Abe was so sad he would talk to no one for a long time. He finally went back to the legislature. He also passed the test to become a lawyer. Then he met Mary Todd. They were married and Abe was soon elected to Congress.

7

Questions and Activities

ABRAHAM LINCOLN

Discussion Questions

1. Abe Lincoln loved his mother very much. When she died he was very sad. He was also very close to his sister and she died, too. When he lost his friend Ann Rutledge, his grief was almost too much. Have you ever had someone die that you loved?

2. Even though Abraham loved his mother very much, he called his step-mother his "best friend." Can you think of any reasons why he was so fond of her?

3. Abe was arrested once because a ferryboat company from Kentucky accused him of running his boat in places where he wasn't allowed. Can you think of any reason why the company accused him of this? Remember that the judge decided that what Abe did was okay.

4. Abraham Lincoln earned the nickname of "Honest Abe" because he was always honest. Can you think of anything you heard or read in this story that would answer why people called him that?

5. President Lincoln disliked slavery very much. He believed that all men should be equal. But he also tried to hold both sides together during the Civil War. Why would he do this when he was against slavery?

6. Abraham Lincoln was a good President. He was also one of the greatest Americans that ever lived. Why would anyone want to kill him?

Activities

1. Have an Honest Abe Day where each student relates to the rest of the class a situation where he was completely honest, even though the honesty might have brought on consequences.

2. Place the silhouette of Abraham on the time line in its appropriate place.

3. Show children a historical map of the North and South as they existed during the Civil War. Explain to them the tragedies of a nation at war with itself.

4. Celebrate Lincoln's birthday (February 12) with a birthday cake. During the party explain to the children the reasons which they can understand for Lincoln being called one of our greatest Presidents.

5. Create a bulletin board with the title "All Men Are Created Equal." Place pictures on the board that show men and women of various ethnic and racial backgrounds together in work, play, singing, and other activities. Explain to children the meaning of the words.

HONEST RAIL SPLITTER

ABRAHAM LINCOLN

HONEST ABE

GEORGE WASHINGTON

Theodore Roosevelt

Theodore Roosevelt was born in New York City on October 27, 1858. He had one brother and two sisters. Theodore loved to play with his family.

But he had an illness called *asthma*. It made him tired and he could not play for very long. His father told him he would get better when he was older. He made up his mind to be strong.

1

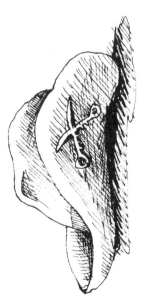

12

Vocabulary

asthma

tutor

politics

assassinated

conservation

safari

mourned

Resources

Teddy Roosevelt, All-Round Boy, Parks.

Theodore Roosevelt, Man of Action, Beach.

Theodore Roosevelt, Hancock.

Notes to Adults

Children will admire the courage of young Theodore Roosevelt as he overcame his childhood affliction with asthma. It was his love of nature and the great outdoors that inspired him to condition his body back to good health.

He led a colorful and rich life as a cowboy, a soldier, an explorer and a politician. His years in the White House were no different. Roosevelt's life represents the full spectrum of honesty, courage and good common sense. Children like to associate with their heroes.

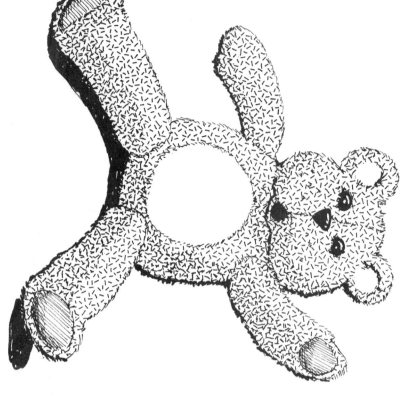

When he retired from his job as President, he returned to Sagamore Hill to relax. He loved travel and adventure. So he took a *safari* into the jungles of Africa. Later he went to South America to explore more jungles. His boat travelled down the danger- ous river of Doubt. No white man had been there before. Theodore became sick with jungle fever. He never was well again. When he died, Americans *mourned* the death of a great President.

Teddy wasn't strong enough to go to school, so he had a *tutor* help him to learn. He loved to read adventure books. Stories about cowboys and pirates were his favorites. He wished he could someday have a horse of his own. He also missed going to school with his friends. These things made him want to get well even more.

3

Roosevelt was elected governor of New York. He then became Vice President under President William McKinley. When McKinley was *assassinated,* Theodore became President of the United States. He was a very popular President and served his country for seven years. He brought honesty to the government and was always friendly to the people. Theodore loved nature and started many *conservation* programs. Five new national parks were started when he was President.

10

His father bought him a pony when he was nine years old. Sometimes he was well enough to ride his pony. He couldn't see very well, so his father took him to an eye doctor. The doctor said Teddy needed glasses. When he got his new glasses, then Teddy could see a lot more of the beauty in the world around him.

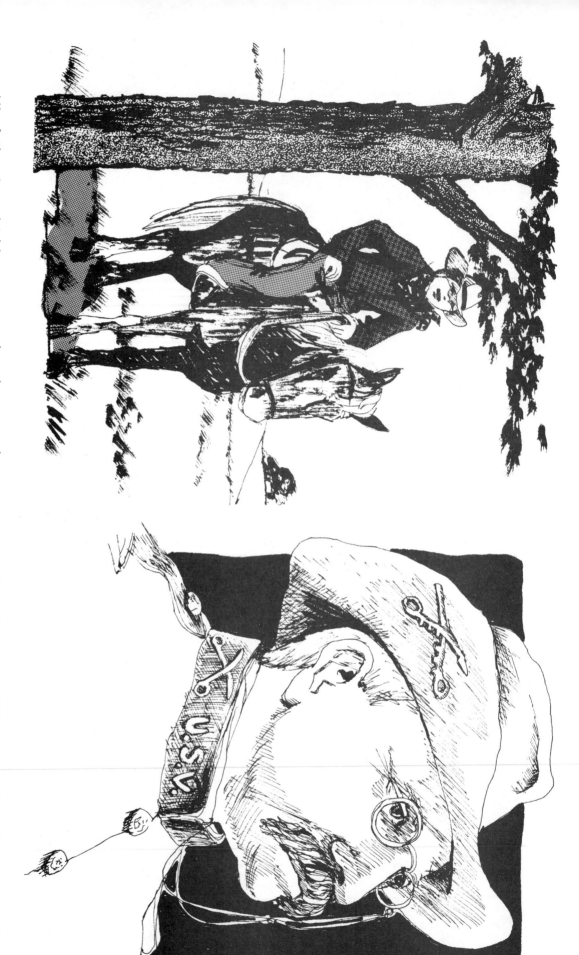

Theodore joined the army when Cuba was trying to win its freedom from Spain. He led a group of men called the Rough Riders. They rode horses and won many important battles in Cuba against the Spanish. Their courage helped Cuba win its independence. When the war was over Theodore came home. He was honored by America as a hero.

Once he went to camp. Some of the boys teased him because he was so weak. He tried to fight back, but he lost. His father built him a gym in their house so Teddy could build up his strength. The gym had weights and bars and a punching bag. Teddy worked very hard to become strong. Finally, he became a healthy and strong man.

When he came back, he married Edith Carow. She had been his friend when they were children. They took his daughter with them and moved into a beautiful house called Sagamore Hill. They had five children of their own. Theodore was a good father. He spent many hours playing with his children in their yard.

Theodore then went to school and learned. He went to Harvard University and studied history and law. He was popular with the other students. After college he married Alice Lee. Theodore then decided to go into *politics*. His honesty helped him become a state senator. His wife then had a baby and died the next day. His mother died a few hours later on the same day. Theodore was overcome with grief.

6

He left his little daughter with his sister and went West to buy a ranch. Theodore learned how to be a cowboy. He stayed there for two years. The adventures he faced were like living out his boyhood dreams. When he came back from the ranch, he was ready to return to politics. Theodore was no longer so sad.

7

30

Questions and Activities

THEODORE ROOSEVELT

Discussion Questions

1. Teddy Roosevelt loved to read about cowboys and pirates. He often daydreamed about adventures he wished he could live. Do you know what it means to daydream? Do you ever daydream?

2. When Theodore Roosevelt was a boy, he promised himself he would work very hard to become strong. Why was it so important to him to become strong?

3. Theodore Roosevelt was one of our most popular Presidents. What was there about him that made him so well-liked?

4. Theodore was cheered as a hero for his work as a leader of the Rough Riders. Why do people have heroes? What made Theodore one of their heroes?

5. Why did Theodore Roosevelt go West to the Dakotas? How did his life change there?

6. After he retired from being President, Theodore made trips to Africa and South America. His friends told him about the dangers of the trip, but Theodore said, "I must go. It's my last chance to be a boy." What did he mean when he said this?

Activities

1. Children will enjoy the story of why Americans affectionately called him "Teddy." One cartoonist drew him with a bear cub. Soon toy makers were producing stuffed animals that came to be known as "Teddy bears." Have children bring their Teddy bears. Discuss with children why Teddy bears are so important to young children.

2. Theodore Roosevelt loved nature and wildlife, and he instituted several conservation programs while he was President. Show children a map of other national parks and discuss with them the purpose of our national park program.

3. Create a bulletin board honoring Theodore Roosevelt. Include pictures that represent important phases of Roosevelt's life. Place a picture of Mt. Rushmore on the board and talk with children about the four faces and the wonders of the monument itself.

4. It took a lot of courage and hard work to overcome his physical condition as a child. Discuss with children the other personality traits he possessed that made him one of our most loved and greatest Presidents.

5. Roosevelt once said about his family living in the White House, "I don't think any family ever enjoyed the White House more than we have." There are several humorous stories about their experiences there. Read to the children some of these stories purely for their listening pleasure and enjoyment.

31

Woodrow Wilson

Thomas Woodrow Wilson was born on December 28, 1856, in Staunton, Virginia. His father was a minister. He was called Tommy as a boy. His family moved to Georgia when he was two years old.

The Civil War was going on during his early years. It was hard for Tommy to understand why men would want to fight against each other. He would someday lead his country through another terrible war.

1

Vocabulary

cotton gin
loft
constitution
debates
ruins
enrolled
popular
accomplished

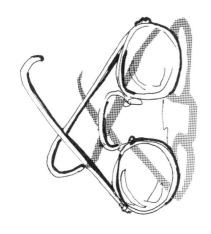

Resources

Woodrow Wilson, Boy President, Monsell.
Story of the Presidents, Petersham.
They Lived in the White House, Cavanah.

12

Notes to Adults

Woodrow Wilson is another person who overcame weakness and poor health to aspire to the presidency. Children will relate to his boyhood experiences in Augusta, Georgia, where his national tendencies as a leader began to emerge. He always stood by his own beliefs, even though he sometimes faced great odds.

Perhaps his greatest disappointment in life was bringing his country into war, because Woodrow Wilson abhorred war and felt men could and should settle their differences in other ways. Following the war he devoted all his energies toward the League of Nations, and he was very disappointed when the Senate refused to ratify United States membership.

He felt that nations could talk out their problems and never have to go to war again. His plan was popular with the people in Europe. But the United States was tired of dealing with Europe's problems. The Senate refused to approve the United States' becoming a member. Woodrow Wilson will always be remembered, though, as a President who ac-*complished* many things because of the way he could talk to people.

Tommy loved Monday more than any other day of the week. His father would take him places he had never been before. While they walked, Tommy could ask his father any question he wanted. He learned a lot from his father. One Monday they went to a gin mill and saw how the *cotton gin* worked. It picked the seeds from the cotton.

3

In 1912 he got his chance. After a hard fought battle, he became the choice of the Democratic Party. Wilson easily won the election. He served two terms as President. He tried to keep our country out of World War I. But when we were drawn into the war, he made a decision as President that made sure we won the war. When the war was over, he worked very hard to get countries to join a League of Nations.

10

Tommy was thin as a boy, and he wasn't very strong. But he loved to play with his friend Joe in the forest. The boys picked blackberries and played Indians and rode horses. Tommy also loved to play with his sisters. He spent many hours having fun with them. The playing usually ended with cookies as a treat from their mother.

After college Woodrow Wilson married Ellen Louise Axson. They had three daughters. He wrote books and taught history at Bryn Mawr College. He then became president of Princeton University. Later Woodrow ran for governor of New Jersey and he won. His powerful speeches made him the *popular* choice of the people. Woodrow Wilson began to think about becoming President of the United States.

As Tommy grew older he began to love to play baseball. He and his friends played baseball whenever they could. One day when it was raining, they went into the *loft* in Tommy's barn. They decided to form a boys' club. The club was called The Lightfoot Club. The club held secret meetings. They elected Tommy president. He had learned from his father about the rules to run meetings. He taught the boys about all the rules.

5

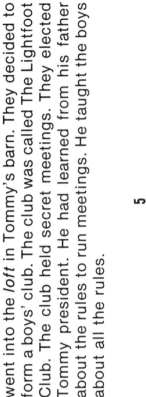

He tried to start college at Davidson when he was seventeen, but the doctors sent him home because he was sick. When he was well he *enrolled* at Princeton. He studied history and government. He became editor of the school newspaper. He began to think about what he wanted to do after college. Tommy decided he might like to become a senator or a governor. But the name Senator Tommy Wilson didn't sound right. So he started being called by his middle name, and he became Woodrow Wilson, the man.

8

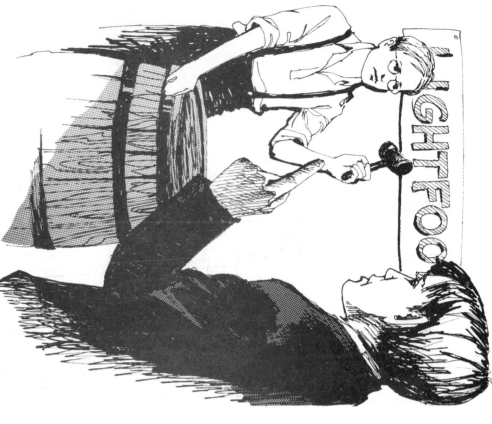

His ability as a leader began to show. The boys asked him to write a *constitution* for the club. Tommy always seemed to be able to get the other boys to see things his way. He was not loud, and he did not give orders. It was the way he said things that always seemed to make sense. Tommy always tried to stand up for the rights of other people. The Lightfoot Club became interested in *debates*. They spent many hours debating both sides of many issues.

Tommy was very sad when his father took a job teaching in Columbia, South Carolina. It meant he would have to leave Augusta and his friends in The Lightfoot Club. He said good-bye to all his friends and went to meet his father who had gone ahead. When he first saw Columbia, he saw only burned out buildings and weeds. The city was in *ruins* from the Civil War. Tommy never forgot Augusta, but he soon became busy with his new life in Columbia.

Questions and Activities

WOODROW WILSON

Discussion Questions

1. When Tommy was a little boy, he liked Mondays better than any other day of the week. Why were Mondays so special to him?

2. Can you think of any reasons for the boys in Tommy's club calling their group The Lightfoot Club?

3. How was Tommy always able to get his friends to see things the way he wanted to see them? Why do you think this quality is important in a leader?

4. Why was Tommy so sad when he left Augusta, Georgia, to live in Columbia, South Carolina? How would you feel if your family moved to another city?

5. Why did Tommy decide to stop using his name Tommy and use his name Woodrow instead?

6. When World War I was over, Woodrow Wilson worked very hard to bring about the League of Nations. Why was it so important to him?

Activities

1. As a boy Woodrow Wilson lived in Georgia during the time of the Civil War. Show the children a map of the United States at that time and point to Georgia as a southern state which actually withdrew from the Union. Tell them of the mixed emotions his family felt and how, even though their loyalties were with the South, they were glad to see the Union survive.

2. Aside from playing baseball, the members of The Lightfoot Club enjoyed doing other things together. They developed a keen interest in the skill of debating. Explain to the children how the subject of any debate must have two sides which can be argued. Talk with them about topics in their young lives which they feel have more than one side.

3. The League of Nations lasted only a short period of time due mainly to the United States not joining its ranks. Explain to the children the reasons why the Senate refused to ratify our membership and how hard President Wilson tried to get us to join. Explain also how, even though the League failed, the United Nations was formed after World War II. Talk about the reason for its existence and the goals it hopes to accomplish.

4. Create a bulletin board in honor of Woodrow Wilson. Have children draw pictures that show the phases of his life which they would have enjoyed most. The board should also include pictures relating to World War I and the League of Nations (or its successor, the United Nations).

Franklin D. Roosevelt

Franklin D. Roosevelt was President of the United States for more than twelve years. That's longer than anyone has ever been President. He was elected four times.

He was born in 1882 in Hyde Park, New York. He was an only child. His parents owned a beautiful home along the Hudson River called Springwood. It had more than 30 rooms.

Vocabulary

schedule
polio
governess
companion
predicted
paralyzed
campaigned
Depression

NEW DEAL

CCC   CWA
PWA
WPA FERA
NYA
WRA

Resources

Franklin Roosevelt, Boy of the Four Freedoms, Weil.
Real Book About Franklin D. Roosevelt, Merriam.

Franklin D. Roosevelt (signature)

Notes to Adults

Franklin D. Roosevelt served as President longer than any man ever has and ever will. Perhaps for this reason alone, Roosevelt would be one of our most well-remembered Presidents. But there is a real hero's story behind his courageous struggles to overcome polio. The controversy associated with his New Deal in bringing the country out of the Great Depression also makes his life interesting reading for children of all ages.

Franklin became known all over the country by his initials FDR. He called his program to help the country his New Deal. FDR created many new programs that gave jobs to people who were out of work. President Roosevelt was so popular with the people that he was elected President three more times! No one else has been chosen President four times. He died shortly after being elected the fourth time, but he had served his country for more than twelve years. FDR will always be remembered as one of our greatest Presidents.

When he was a boy, Franklin loved to watch the boats go up and down the Hudson River. He decided then he wanted to be a sailor when he grew up. His mother had a very strict *schedule* for Franklin to follow. Both of his parents were careful not to spoil Franklin.

By then Franklin was famous all over the United States. The Democrats asked him to run for President. He worked very hard and *campaigned* in almost all the states. He wanted to show the people that his handicap would not stop him from being a good President. He was elected by a large number of votes. People put their trust in him to help the country at a time when many had no jobs and no money. The time was called the Great *Depression*.

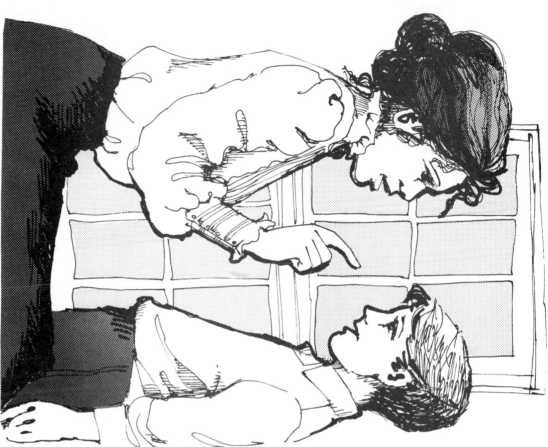

Franklin's parents began taking him on trips with them to Europe when he was very young. He did not go to schools like we know schools. He had teachers who taught just him. They were called tutors. Franklin also learned much from his governess. He was a very smart boy and learned quickly.

Franklin spent several months each year at Warm Springs, Georgia. Many people with polio had been helped by swimming in its waters. Mr. Roosvelt liked it there and bought the land so people who did not have much money could have free treatments. He then ran for governor of New York and won. People admired his courage in fighting back from his illness. They also liked his honesty.

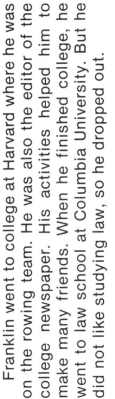

Franklin went to college at Harvard where he was on the rowing team. He was also the editor of the college newspaper. His activities helped him to make many friends. When he finished college, he went to law school at Columbia University. But he did not like studying law, so he dropped out.

One day Franklin was sailing and fell into the water. He became chilled. The next day he felt very tired. His legs had no feeling. Doctors found out that he had a disease called *polio*. It made his legs *paralyzed* and Franklin could not walk. He worked very hard, trying to fight against the illness. He swam a lot to make his arms and shoulders strong. Finally, he was able to drag himself along with the help of braces.

Franklin had known his distant cousin Eleanor Roosevelt since their childhood. He and Eleanor made plans to marry. Franklin's mother did not want her son to marry anyone, but they got married anyway. They had six children. Franklin was a good father and *companion* to his children. He loved to swim and sail and play with them.

The Democratic Party leaders asked Franklin to run for the New York Senate. He was *not predicted* to win, but he called for clean government. He won an upset election. President Woodrow Wilson appointed Franklin Assistant Secretary of the Navy. Franklin was very happy with his new job because he could be near ships and the water.

Questions and Activities

FRANKLIN D. ROOSEVELT

Discussion Questions

1. Why do you think Franklin's parents were careful not to spoil him when he was a child?

2. Why was Franklin so overjoyed when he was appointed Assistant Secretary of the Navy?

3. Franklin D. Roosevelt will always be remembered as one of our most courageous Presidents. What do you think is the most courageous thing he ever did?

4. Why do you think Franklin D. Roosevelt bought Warm Springs, Georgia, and started the Warm Springs Foundation?

5. Once Franklin D. Roosevelt became President, he became better known by his initials "FDR." Why do you think people called him this instead of his name?

6. What did FDR do to help bring the country out of the Great Depression?

Activities

1. Franklin Roosevelt was born in his parents' mansion called Springwood. It had over 30 rooms. If possible, show children a picture of the sprawling estate and allow them to offer suggestions and speculate what they would do with a house that had over 30 rooms. Encourage them to use their imaginations here.

2. Discuss with children that both President Theodore Roosevelt and Franklin D. Roosevelt had the same last name. Sometimes when people have the same name, it means they are relatives. Have the children cite their own family members as examples. Then explain to them that Theodore and Franklin were in fact distantly related.

3. Explain to children the sadness of the Great Depression. Even though the explanation must be simple, they will be able to understand the trouble that occurs when many people lose their jobs and have no money.

4. Explain to children about how the 22nd Amendment prevents anyone from serving more than two terms or ten years as President. Tell them that FDR was elected four times before this addition to the Constitution.

5. Create an FDR bulletin board, displaying pictures of the many, many important events of his administration.

47

NEW DEAL

CCC
FERA
NYA
WRA

PWA
CWA
TVA
WPA

Franklin D. Roosevelt

WWII

MARCH OF DIMES

NEW DEAL

48

John F. Kennedy

John Fitzgerald Kennedy was born in 1917 in Brookline, Massachusetts. He was the second of nine children in his family. His father and mother were very wealthy and had millions of dollars.

John F. Kennedy was called Jack by everyone. Jack's older brother Joe, Jr., was his best friend. He could do most things better than Jack. That made Jack try even harder.

Vocabulary

vacations
competition
mansion
suburb
pneumonia
ambassador
physical
heroism
glamour
motorcade

Resources

John F. Kennedy, Young Statesman, Frisbee.
The Life and Words of John F. Kennedy, Wood.
Boy's Life of John F. Kennedy, Lee.
John F. Kennedy and PT-109, Tregaskis.

Notes to Adults

John F. Kennedy is always popular among children who study our Presidents. The image of handsome, physically fit youths, which he and his family brought to the White House, adds to children's own ideas of the American dream come true.

Not to be overlooked is the determination Kennedy showed in overcoming his many illnesses and physical problems as well as his bravery and courage displayed in serving his country. Children love to study their heroes, and Kennedy is certainly one of them.

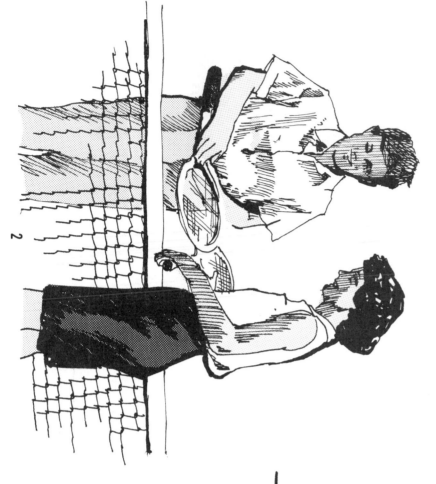

2

On November 22, 1963, President Kennedy was riding in a *motorcade* in Dallas, Texas. He was struck down by an assassin's bullet and died a few hours later. One of the saddest thoughts about his death was that he had not had time to carry out his dreams. John F. Kennedy had great ideas for his country, and his people were making them come true. The whole world mourned his death. He will always be remembered as one of our greatest Presidents, because he brought a new hope to a restless world.

11

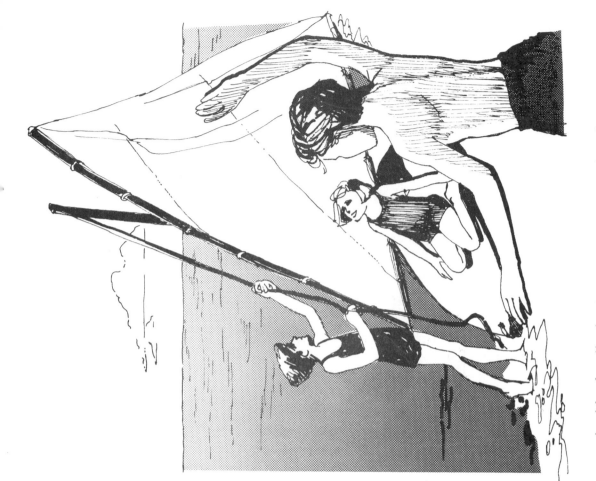

Jack's family had a summer vacation home on Cape Cod. They also had a winter home in Florida. The Kennedy's always had a lot of fun visiting these homes during their *vacations*. They loved to play together. Jack's favorite times were when his family was on vacation.

3

John F. Kennedy's name became well-known all over the country. The Democrats chose him to run for President in 1960. He won a very close election over Richard Nixon and became the youngest ever elected President. The Kennedy's brought a new spirit and *glamour* to the White House. The nation looked to his new leadership to carry them through. He created the Peace Corps to help people in other countries. Kennedy also launched the space program, and he always fought for the equal rights of all people. Jack Kennedy was a very popular President.

10

Jack's parents encouraged competition among their children. Jack's brother Joe was two years older. It seemed like Joe could always run faster, fight harder and play baseball better. But this did not make Jack sad. It made him try to be as good as Joe. Jack admired his brother very much. Their father wanted his children to be as prepared for the grown-up world as he was. He had made a fortune because he was competitive and never gave up.

In 1946 John F. Kennedy ran for Congress. He worked very hard and won the election. In Congress he brought up many good ideas that earned the respect of the other Congressmen. After three terms in the House of Representatives, Kennedy ran for the U.S. Senate. Most people did not expect him to win, but his hard work paid off and he did win. The next year he married Jacqueline Lee Bouvier. She was very beautiful and came from a high society family. Their marriage was a huge social event. They had two children, Caroline and John.

Young Jack always went to private schools. When he was in the fourth grade, his family moved to a brick *mansion* in a *suburb* near New York City. Nurses and servants looked after the children. Jack joined the Boy Scouts and went on overnight hikes along the Hudson River. When he was thirteen he left home to go to a Catholic school in Connecticut. He was homesick but he loved the sports there. Jack really liked to play football best of all.

5

After college Jack tried to get into both the Army and the Navy. But his back injury did not let him pass the *physical*, so he went home and did exercises to make his back strong. Jack passed the physical and joined the Navy. He became an officer and commanded a boat called the PT-109. His boat was destroyed by the enemy. Jack helped to save the lives of his men and find their way to safety. He was given medals for his *heroism*.

8

Jack and his close friends at school called themselves the Muckers. They had a lot of fun together and often played pranks on other students. While at Choate school he became very ill with *pneumonia*. But he finally recovered and went on to graduate. His grades were not very good. But his classmates voted him the man most likely to succeed later in life.

He went to college at Harvard. Jack was on the swimming team and played football, too. During a football practice he hurt his back. His back would bother him the rest of his life. While Jack was still in college, his father became *ambassador* to Great Britain. He asked Jack and Joe to go to Europe to report to him about any trouble there. Jack came back and wrote a book on what he had seen. The book became a best seller. Jack Kennedy graduated with honors from Harvard.

Questions and Activities

JOHN F. KENNEDY

Discussion Questions

1. How did Jack Kennedy's boyhood days help him to become a man who never gave up?

2. The Kennedys were a big family who all loved sports, and they loved to play games together. Why do you think sports were so important to the Kennedys?

3. Jack's older brother Joe always wanted to become President someday. Can you think of any reason how this might have helped Jack to want to be President too?

4. John F. Kennedy was always a man of courage. Tell some examples in his life where he showed a lot of courage and was brave.

5. President Kennedy and his wife Jacqueline brought a new image and spirit to the White House. Why were they so popular among the American people?

Activities

1. Create a Jack Kennedy bulletin board. There are many now-famous photographs of his boyhood days that will stimulate interest in Kennedy as a youth. Discuss with children the youthful, exuberant spirit he and his family carried with them into the White House—a spirit that made them so popular with the people. Children will not learn this from the short story, but it should be discussed with them.

2. Read the children the story of Kennedy's heroism following the Battle of the Solomon in which the PT-109 was destroyed by the Japanese. Show them a picture of the boat if possible and explain his courage in saving his men.

3. Because of the popularity of President Kennedy, many places have been named and renamed in his honor. Make a list with the children of some of these places which now bear the memory of his name.

4. Mention is made of Kennedy's Peace Corps in the story. Talk with the children about its goals and accomplishments over the years. Explain how it was one of Kennedy's achievements mainly because of the thousands of young Americans who gave up their time and talent to serve the country abroad.

5. One of President Kennedy's most famous quotes was "Ask not what your country can do for you. Ask what you can do for your country." Discuss this with children and ask them what it means to them. What can they as young Americans do for their country?